Erasmus W. Reed

Civil War Letters of Erasmus W. Reed

Company B, 9th Pennsylvania infantry, 1861-1864

Erasmus W. Reed

Civil War Letters of Erasmus W. Reed
Company B, 9th Pennsylvania infantry, 1861-1864

ISBN/EAN: 9783337410384

Printed in Europe, USA, Canada, Australia, Japan

Cover: Foto ©ninafisch / pixelio.de

More available books at **www.hansebooks.com**

CIVIL WAR LETTERS OF ERASMUS W. REED,

COMPANY B, 9TH PENNSYLVANIA INFANTRY,

1861-1864

Hazel River, Va. 74 2 5

January 27th, 1863

Dear Parents, Brothers and Sisters:

Your letter of the 23rd reached me this evening enjoying good health. I trust this will find you all in the same good condition. There is nothing new or interesting going here at present. The reenlistment excitement has passed over. All those that wanted to go in for another three year term have done so and are waiting their turns to go home on thirty day furlough. You need have no fears of me being so foolish. I have lost three precious <u>years</u> and am now without a trade. But if God gives me my health, I have hopes yet to make up for it.

By the time I will come home Andrew will be of age and likewise master of his trade, and if you then want another apprentice I am at your disposal. I will commence where I left off when I entered the army. That is, call myself 20 years (old) and go to work. My ambition is to be a good mechanic. Such are my plans for the future, if <u>God</u> is willing.

It grieves me very much to hear that George is or has turned out so bad. <u>God</u> pity <u>him</u>. How is Uncle John Reed getting along? And I am also surprised and sorry to hear of Is Spancake's bad doings. He had better joined the army here (age), where the temptations are not quite so plenty. He might have made a third class man here. Really I am very sorry for Is. I would like to see all former friends turn out well.

Last evening we were off serenading to Division headquarters. Captain Luning, the Division quarter master got married and it was him we serenaded. Our band is improving very rapidly. We got praises every where we play. The furlough business is stopped on account of so many reenlisted being absent from the army, had it not been for that I have no doubt but what I could have got home. Well, only 7 months more. The mince pies you sent me were glorious. They could not have been better. They had not lost any of their original taste. With much love to you all I will close. Write soon again.

Your Affectionate Son

E.W. Reed

July 26th, 1862
Harrison Landing

Dear Parents, Brothers and Sisters:

Having a leisure for a few moments this evening I will improve it in writing to you. I am enjoying very good health and this leaves me with all love to those will send you all enjoying the same great blessing. I have not heard from you since last week. I am anxious to hear from you. I also sent for a shirt in one of my former letters. But it has not come to hand yet and I did not know whether you recieved it or not. The shirt would come very handy if I had it. If you have not sent it until this comes to hand, leave the end seam (of the parcel) open, it will not cost as much and is just as safe.

There is not much news here, we were on picket yesterday and returned today noon. There was everything quiet along the line, no firing like we used to have up at Fairfax. The pickets were firing at each other all the time. But I thought it was the hottest day we have had yet. We went between three and four miles. We were doing duty on a splendid farm with large corn fields. The corn is not quite ripe enough yet. I must now close for this time. I heard the other day that the small pox was in town. I hope you will be very careful in regard to that disease. My love to you all. Write soon and a long letter.

Your loving Son and Brother

L. W. Reed

P.S. Direct as usual. I wrote to Hester Ann but have recieved no answer yet.

In camp near Stafford Court House, Va.

Dear Parents, Brothers and Sisters:

Your letter dated the 18th came duly to hand this evening. Its contents were perused with pleasure. I am well and fondly hope that this will reach you all in the same good condition. Nothing new has transpired since I wrote to you from this place, which by the tenor of your letter you had not received up to the time of your writing.

We are still in the same camp. The rebels hold Fredricksburg yet and no doubt mean to show fight in that vicinity. But I do not think our Generals mean to advance on Richmond in that direction, because it may cost a considerable number of lives before we get to our main object, and that is Richmond. We cannot afford to lose anybody until we get there. They might ship us to a point nearer the city and also then be in communication with our General Boals. We must take Richmond this time or the property holders in the north will get crazy.

Several/fellows of our fellows got letters in the company stating that all the talk at home is the soldiers are getting too much pay. Ain't that encouraging for us? Why the fools! Think they that we are out here by contract and enduring all these hardships for the poor pittance of $13 per month, and which, blast them, they seem to forget that those of us that survive the war must help to pay in taxes, regardless of what we have sacrificed for the country.

Was it us or they that brought the war upon us? No, the rebels caused the war and it was God's will that it should be so. We have it upon us and must make the best of it we can. It appears also that the complaint is the army had not done enough. My God! How could we do more? Have we not been at (it) almost day and night?

Our gains over the enemy should tell them that we have not worked for nothing. We have taken from the rebels 3/4 of Virginia and nearly the whole sea coast. But because we were overpowered and could not take

Richmond they condemn us. I have been so mad at times reading the different accounts from home, that were it not that the innocent would suffer with the guilty, I could have wished the war into the very heart of my own native state. Then the sneaking, money hungry varmints would get an idea of war. Aye it would become impressed upon their very hearts because their heart's idol would be taken from them - their property.

Too much pay indeed! Why, they do not think it too much to pay from five hundred to a thousand dollars for substitutes when they were drafted six months (ago). Money was no object then, when their precious bodys were to be exposed as a target for rebels. And And I would also advise them to recollect that we must help to pay the handsome bounties they paid the last volunteers, so that the draft would not take so many.

We old tropps can at least lay our hands on our hearts and say we did not come out for money, but our love of country brought us here, and not the $13 and one hundred dollar bounty that we were to recieve at the expiration of the war. Would it be a wonder if we were discouraged with our friends, the politicians in the north, and the rebels in the south fighting against us?

God grant that we will be victorious in the next battles and Richmond will be taken so that war will come to an end. I am sick and tired of it. There is no more honor in defending one's country and our services are not appreciated.

I recieved the gloves and tobacco you sent me and am very much obliged for it. We have still had no pay day. But I don't care for any money here in this Heaven forsaken place. The weather in day time is not very cold but the nights are biting. I understand we are to (have) the shelter tents. We will get cold noses in them as they are only made of thin muslin. I must close with the hope that with God's help our troubles will end soon. I send my love to you all and remain

Your Affectionate Son

E. W. Reed

Write soon and be careful in your direction

Headquarters 96th Regt. P.V.

Camp Northumberland   Jan. 9th

Beloved Parents, Brothers and Sisters:

Being at leisure for a few moments this evening I concluded to write you this letter. In the first place I will tell you that I am enjoying very good health, and I sincerely hope you are all enjoying the same Blessing. I recieved your present last evening and I was very glad to recieve it. It came quite unexpected, because I did not expect it till Sam Filbert came here. But you will accept my heartfelt thanks. You will please give my thanks to Mrs Kendel for her presents to me. Luxuries are scarce out here.

I have a little news for you this time. The other day I was detailed for special duty at Brigade headquarters and on coming over there I was ordered to go with the teams. I did not know where we were going till they told me that we were going to Mount Vernon. You may think that I was glad enough to go there to visit the resting place of the Father of our country.

The place is about 12 miles below Alexandria. We went down for some straw. We got the straw about 1/4 of a mile from the house on the Mount Vernon farm. After we had loaded we went over to see the place. I first visited the flour (flower) gardens, then the tomb. It is a vault about 10 feet square, with an iron door in front, that is an iron grate door, so that everybody can look in. The coffin of Washington is on the right hand side as you come there and his wife's coffin on the left. The coffins are composed of marble stone, very large. I then went to the house and seen some old relics. The key of the Bastile, presented to Washington by Lafayette. I would not have missed that trip for anything.

We returned home just as it was getting dark. I will also let you know that we recieved new rifles the other day. They are a bully gun. We used to have the old muscat (musket) until then. About our pay. They have fooled us again. We are expecting the pay master around here every day. It is the general opinion around here that the Colonel keeps our pay back, because all the other regiments get payed off every two months. Our hope is we will get payed as all the regiments in our Brigade are not payed yet. But you can look for my money.

If Andrew has got the enlisting fever yet I would advise him not to enlist, because we don't get one half what was promised us. I have no doubt there will be plenty of recruiters around and they will promise all sort of things that you don' t get. And above all, not in a strange company. Because (I) have seen a little how things are managed. If a man joins a strange company he is only a dog. Nobody will look after him when he is sick. And in other (ways) I would advise the yound men that are at home to stay there. Our Regiment is a regular darn humbug with such a Colonel. But you must not take at the above writing that I am tired of soldier's life for I am not. Uncle Sam treats his boys right. It's only the officers. But I must come to a close. Write soon and let me know all the news. Israel is well. Give my respects to all friends. So no more. My love to you all .

Remaining Your Loving Son

E.W. Reed

Direct to me Co. b, 96th Regiment P.V.

In care of Captain P.A. Filbert

Alexandria Fairfax County Va.

January 2, 1862
Headquarters 96th Regiment P.V.
Camp Northumberland, (Va.)

Beloved Parents, Brothers and Sisters:

Your letter was recieved about five minutes back and having nothing to do I thought I would answer it immediately. In the first place I will say that I am enjoying fully good health and have enjoyed the same ever since I am a soldier. I have gained about 20 to 25 pounds in weight since we are away from Pottsville. Therefore you may think that the life I lead agrees with me.

We just returned from picket last night. We were out about 10 miles from our camp and were gone five days. We did not see much of the rebels but we were twice alarmed, the first time at half past one o'clock in the nigh We were on the outpost. One of the sentinels fired and then another one, and afterwards a general volley of four guns, which was the signal to get ready. About one half of the company was sleeping and the rest on their posts or around the fire. But when the alarm was given every man was in his place in two or three minutes, with guns cocked and ready. But after about a half an hour, it was found out that the rebels had either gone off or it was something else had disturbed the sentinel. But we expected an attack. But the rebels did not come so we had nothing to fight. But the quarters are back on picket.

It was just like coming home to a house when we came to our snug little log cabins. We have 2 blankets apiece. That makes 12 blankets for our mess, so you may consider that we sleep warm. The weather has not (been) very cold yet this far. As for snow, that is quite out of question, because we have not had any yet. Of course we have had some pretty cool nights, but in the day time it is nearly always warm.

About liking it (I) must say that I like it first rate. Day after tomorrow we will have pay day and as you spoke in your letter about Sam Filbert coming out, I will send the money with him. I wish you would let me know what you are working at this winter and everything. And another thing is I

do not want you at home to trouble yourselves about me, because I think
that it has been to my benefit all along. If it is God's will it is my opinion that we will be at home till (by) the 4th of July. The movements of the
armies all around indicates as much. Anyhow the rebels will have to give up
soon. I want Andrew to stick to the band. And ask Uncle Jake why he don't answer my letters. But I must bring my letter to a close, hoping/this comes
home it will find you all in very good health and in good spirits.

I wonder what All Manwiller said when he recieved his 15 letters all
in one mail and none paid. We done it just for a joke. But I will stop writing for this time as it is nearly roll call. Give my respects to Dr. Dreher
and Marry, also to all the friends. My love to you all. No more, but write
soon as I am always anxious to hear from you. My love to all my brothers and
sisters.

From Your Affectionate Son

E.W. Reed

We are in winter quarters quartered in our new cabins.
P.S. You may expect the money with Sam Filbert and if he don't come soon I
will try and send it some other way.
Direct to me Company B, 96th Regiment, P.V.
In care of Captain P.A. Filbert
Alexandria
Fairfax County
Virginia

Beloved Parents, Brothers and Sisters:

Yours of 16th came duly to hand and was perused with pleasure, as it in formed me that you were well at home. I am also well and I hope by the time this reaches you it will still find you enjoying good health. I would have written before this, but I expected to be payed every day and as the paymaster has not made his appearance yet I thought you would get uneasy, so I concluded to write.

There is something wrong about our pay but no one seems to know rightly what it is. But this much we do know, that the Colonel has kept our pay back for some kind of a private speculation. The excuse now is that we would have to wait till the last ones, because it would take so much gold and silver, being that so many had made allotments at home, that is Pottsville, and the man that forwards the money there wants the gold. So I do not exactly know what day we will get payed, but it cannot go long any more. The General has taken the affair into his hands. The Regiment is very dissatisfied with the Colonel. He is a mean rascal.

The weather is very unpleasant just now. It has been rainy weather for the last week. The mud in our streets is five or six inches deep, and all around is nothing but mud. Our company recieved that box of stockings from Pine Grove. They were very welcome. We also got a keg of peper sause (pepper sauce) from Mr. Filbert. It was also gladly recieved. It is made pretty much like our cold sallow (cole slaw).

There is nothing particular going on just now. I seen in the paper today that we have gained a great victory in Kentucky. Bully for that. There will be some heavy blows struck thick and fast. It is supposed that the war will be over in a month or so. We all hope it will, and peace and harmony once more restored to our country. About sending me another box. You would better wait till I send or write for it, because I do not know how long we will stay here. Then if we would not be here any more it would be lost. Of course I am not sure of moving, but at a time like this we do not know what day we may get marching orders. But I must bring my letter to a close. You can look for my money any day, for we do not know what day the pay master my may drop in and give us our shino. So no more for this time, but hoping to hear from you soon, and more than that to be home soon myself, I will stop. But give me all the news. My respects to all friends.

Your Loving Son

E.W. Reed

Direct to me Company B, 96th Regiment, P.V..

In care of Captain Filbert, Alexandria, Fairfax County, Va.

P.S. There is still some more good news this evening. I was just out and Steesy (?) tells me that the press has it that the rebels are retreating from Manassas Junction. I hope it is true. And also that the Colonel has said that we would get payed this week. I believe this is the first time he has said we would get payed, so I suppose it is true, for once..

P.S. Andrew, let me know how the band is getting along and please give my respects to them all, and ask Is Spancake the reason he don't answer my letter. And also tell Uncle Jake I thought he was a nice fellow for not answering my letter.

Beloved Parents:

Your welcome letter came to hand this evening and as usual, most joyfully. It reached me in excellent health and my sincere hope is that by the time this reaches you ir will find you all enjoying the same blessing, especially little Ellie. I hope, through God's mercy, she will be entirely recovered.

There is nothing particularly new going on here, except that we have had the photograph of the Regiment taken today, and also that we reciaved marching orders. But as it has again commenced raining, I should not be surprised if it should be postponed. The weather had been quite pleasant for a few days, but it appears the weather is not settled yet. We also had Regimental drill during these fine days. The Regiment does finely, but we are getting tired of this place. We have been here now over two months, so you can imagine we are tired of the mud ~~puddles~~ puddles. But I like the soldier's life yet. But I am getting half tired of the bean soup. We have had bean soup now for nearly one month regular every dinner.

I have been down to Alexandria three times since we are on this side of the river. It is a fine old place. But there are a good many rank se~~ceshix~~ ceshies (secessionists) in the place. The war now are glorious. Nashville is occupied by our troops and the morning paper states that the white flag is waving over Memphis and depend upon it that are long the ~~stars~~ stars and stripes will float over Richmond.

The ~~report~~ report that the Governor of Tennessee has ordered all their soldiers to lay down their arms is also confirmed. Therefore the rebels will have so many the less. I should think that the recent victories has rather dampened their ardor. By March their twelve months' soldiers time will have expired. I have no doubt the most of them will take advantage of it and go to their homes. By May it is considered the rebellion will have been crushed entirely out of the ~~land~~ country. Then won't there be a jubilee and rejoicing all through the land! But I must come to a close. I send my undying love to you, my parents, and all my brothers and sisters. Write soon.

Your Loving Son and Brother

E.W. Reed

Direct the same as before. My regards to all the friends.

(On the back page of the same letter.)

To Mary, Eliza, Clementine, George, Willie and Ellen:

Your letter was gladly recieved. It made me feel xx happy to
hear that you were progressing so well in school. I hope by the time I will
come home, which if God spares my life will not be far distant, to see you,
Clementine, Eliza, Georgy and Willie, educated young ladies and gentlemen.
But I can't write much this evening. I sppose you will hear what is written
on the other pages, so no more. My love to you all.

Your Brother

E.W. Reed

March 6th 1862

Camp Northumberland, Va.

Beloved Parents:

You will no doubt be surprised to recieve a letter from me in our old camp. Last evening we got marching orders at Fairfax and march-
But
ed back to camp last night. But we are not to stay here more than a day or two. We will either move south to North Carolina or reinforce Burnside or go west, I cannot tell you for certain in this letter. The main bulk of the army is staying at Manassas and vicinity to operate there. I will let you know of our where abouts as soon as possible.

' That was a great retreat of the rebels leaving their much boasted stronghold at Manassas, Bull Run and Centreville. We have got every-thing. It is believed that they will not make one other good stand with the whole of our enormous army down on them. Their back bone is broken and a little more struggling and this war will be over, if it be God's will .

We have had very hard marching this last week. I am enjoying very good health and it is my sincere wish and hope that this will reach you all enjoying the same blessing. But I must close for this time. Write soon. My undying love to you all at home.

Your Loving Son

E.W. Reed

Direct to me Company B, 96th Regiment, P.V.

General Slocum's Brigade

Franklin Division

Alexandria

March 9th, 1862
Camp Northumberland, Va.

Beloved Parents:

Your very welcome letter came to hand this evening. It reached me in very good health and it is my sincere hope this will find you all enjoying the same Blessing. There is nothing interesting going on here for the present. The weather is beautiful, in fact I think it is getting summer very fast. The roads are dried off.

By your letter I understand you had thought we were moved. But we are here at the old place yet. We have got orders to keep ourselves in readiness to move at a minute's notice. But we have had that order now for two weeks. Therefore I cannot tell you when we will march.

I was wondering what was the matter that you did not write. You can just send your letters. I am sure to get them. You inquired in your letter what was the reason I sent that blanket and pair of boots home. I do not need them here. I have got one blanket here yet, and it would have made too much of a load to carry. As for the boots, it is getting too hot; we have got leggings and another thing we have now got the small tents, and them we will have to carry in our knapsacks. They are divided in two pieces and two men to a tent. Our Regiment is getting along fine. We have got the finest Regiment in our Division. Our troops have gained another victory. They have taken Leesburg and in every direction our cause is prospering finely. We all expect to be at home in a few months. But I must close for this time. Write soon again. I am always anxious to hear from home. Give my love to Uncle Harry, Aunt Eliza, the Drehers and all the rest. So I will close with sending my love to you and all my brothers and sisters. Hoping to be home soon I will stop.

Your Loving Son

E.W. Reed

Direct your letters to me Company B, 96th Regiment, P.V. in care of Captain P. A. Filbert or Colonel H.L. Cake

White House, Va.

Camp Anthony   May 17th, 1862

Dear Parents, Brothers and Sisters:

The Captain having just told us that the Pine Grove folks
were complaining of not getting any letters from us, so I concluded to write
this letter. I am enjoying bully good health and in good spirits and all that
I wish and hope is that this will reach you all at home in the same good condition.

You will see by the heading of my letter that we have advanced pretty far up the peninsula and there are plenty of troops ahead of us
yet. Day before yesterday we made the march here through mud and rain. It was
a caution, but we had only 5 or 6 miles to go. Today we are almost roasting
from heat. We had got marching orders to march at 12 o'clock but the order
was countermanded.

There are between 50 and 60 thousand troops encamped in the
field around us. It is a splendid sight in the evening. There are not very
many sick in our Regiment. There had been a few sick in our company, but they
are recovering. I think before many days we will be in Richmond and when once
there I have no doubt the war will be ended.

But about you not recieving so many letters any more, you
must not forget the distance we have gone. And another thing is we must wait
for chances to send our letters. You may probably not get this letter in less
than a week. I write at least one letter in a week and most of the time two,
just as I have opportunity. I have recieved no letter from you for some time.
I am anxious to have a letter from home. When you write let me know whether
Sister Emma has gone off. If she has and you write to her, send her my love.
I will write to them. Let me know how you are all individually getting along,
what the girls are doing and the little boys, whether they go to school or
lounge about the shop./I must close for this time. Write very soon, and a long
letter.

Your Loving Son and Brother

My love to you, one and all of you.

March 20th, 1862

Camp Northumberland, Va.

Beloved Parents, Brothers and Sisters:

  Your letter recieved this evening brings me sad news indeed. I am quite disheartened since I read the letter, to think that my poor little Ellie is suffering so. I hope through God's blessing she will have recovered by the time this reaches home. I am not content till I hear from you again, with better news than your last letter contained. This letter leaves me, thank God, enjoying good health. May it please the Lord that this may reach you as it leaves me, enjoying that one of His great blessings.

  I think I mentioned to you in one of my letters that we expected to move last Monday, but we are here yet. It is uncertain when we move again, and as to where, we do not know where we go when we do move. But one thing is certain, that the rebellion race is nearly over. With God's help we are gaining every battle, and one or two more moves will, I think, entirely crush the rebellion.

  Yesterday we had two reviews, one in the forenoon, a brigade review, and in the afternoon we were again reviewed by McClellan, that is, our whole division. There has been nothing particularly new going on since we are again in our old camp. The weather has been fine until today. It commenced raining last night, and has been raining nearly all day. We have spring here and birds of the season are here. It is refreshing to hear their sweet music.

  You mentioned something about coming home. God knows I would gladly come home on a furlough, but it is utterly impossible for me to do so at the present time. By your letter it appears to look very gloomy in Pine Grove. But, my God, how it looks out here! Families driven from their homes! On our march out to Fairfax I got to see a little into the horrors of war. Every place where there was anything to eat, it was taken by the soldiers. Hogs, cattle, chickens were just taken from the very door of families, and killed in their sight. At some places it was, perhaps, the last thing the people had to depend on. I know you will exclaim with me thanks to our Heavenly Father that

this is not carried on in our own peaceful homes in the north. The people
in the north would be worse off if the rebels had driven us back instead of
us driving them

Dear Brother:

I will not have much to say because you can see the letter I sen
to our parents. About the article you are going to send me, I will be secret
with it and send it home again. In your letter you mentioned that you wished
you were with me in the war. You can thank your stars that you are not here.
We have very hard times. The three months' soldiers only had play to what we
have to do. Therefore just put the notion out of your head.

Andrew, it is your duty to stay at home. Maybe you think I write
this way just to make (give) you the horrors. I would not write you any lies.
About you being tired of laying around, work must get brisker this summer
because business will go on again. It is not expected around here that the
war will last longer than April or May. So no more for this time. I wish you
would write sooner. Always

Your Loving Brother

E.W. Reed

April 23rd, 1862
Aboard Ship S.R. Spaulding

Beloved Parents, Brothers and Sisters:

Finding a slight lull in the confusion I thought I would try and write a few lines to you informing you that I am still enjoying very good health, and it is my sincere wish and hope this will reach you all enjoying the same Blessing.

We are now aboard the ships, that is our division, six days. We are laying here as a reserve and it is my candid opinion that we will never see any fighting in this war. We have traveled around a good deal already. The fight at Yorktown will settle the war. The rebels confess that themselves. They say if they lose Yorktown they might as well give up. They took three prisoners to Fort Monroe and they say their officers say so and Yorktown will be taken as sure as there is a dollar in the U.S.A.

We do not know when we will get landed or where. Here we are anchored in Poquoson Bay. But we are getting reconciled to being penned up so. The noise os not quite so much as it was. I suppose the big mouthed fellows have wasted the gas all the first few days. There is lots of oysters here and easy to be got, but we cannot get off the ships to get them.

The boys are all well with the exception of a few complaining. I suppose they are a little seasick. For myself I must say I never felt better. The sea agrees bully with me. But I must close for this time. Write soon.

From Your Loving Son and Brother

E.W. Reed

April, 1862···

Weaverville

Company B, 96th Regiment, Pennsylvania / Volunteers

Dear Parents:

I will again drop a few lines to you,with pleasure informing you that I am enjoying very good health and it is my sincere wish and hope this will reach you enjoying the same Blessing. We have again moved since I last wrote to you and have had very hard times. Our summer has suddenly changed into a very severe winter. The first night we were encamped in a swamp. It was very wet before we came there, and rained all of that night and next day and the night after there was three inches of snow fell. In the morning when we awoke we were sleeping in about four inches of water, all our things wringing wet. Our small (tents) do not do us any good for such kind of weather. We would just as well have nothing.

The next day about dinner we went out in the country to hunt a house. We found one about 1 1/2 (miles) from camp, with the old Secessh at home. He refused to take us in. But we stopped here and are now detailed to guard his property. Then he gave us room in one of his nigger huts and a basement room where I am at this moment writing. The man that lives here owns 11 or 12 hundred acres of land. Some of his slaves are here yet. He also had about a thousand sheep so we lived a little fat. We also had some of Aunt Dinah's hoe cakes, but they charge at the rate of 25 cents a piece for them. They are about as large as a flan cake.

I will also inform you that we got paid here today and you will please find $15 enclosed. I had intended to send you $20. But since we are marching we very often get short of rations as they cannot transport them fast enough and a little money at such times comes handy and saves me from going hungry to sleep. If everything goes on as swimmingly as it did this last week with our army, we may hope that I need not send my money home, but bring it personally. Our General is marching on them from Fortress Monroe and we down this way. But the severe weather has delayed us so I think they will

have the fun xxxx all to themselves. But I must close. You may recollect
that it is our company that is stopping here. The old rebel said today that
he wished the rebels were all in hell. The soldiers are nearly eating him up.
You will please write immediately on receipt of this letter so I know when
you recieve the money. So with my undying love to you all I will close.

                    Your Loving Son

                        E.W. Reed

Direct to me Company B, 96th Regiment P.V.

        2nd Brigade, Franklin's Division, Washington D.C.

            Be careful in directing.

April 27th, 1862

Dear Parents, Brothers and Sisters:

Your letter dated the 19th came duly to hand ~~kxixxxxxxkxg~~ and its contents were perused with great pleasure as it informed me of the good health prevailing at home. I am also enjoying very good health and hope by the time this reaches you it will still find you enjoying the same Blessing. I had been quite anxious to hear from you as I had recieved no letter for nearly two weeks.

I suppose by this time you will have recieved some of my letters written aboard ship. I wrote two while there. We are at present on terra firma again. That is, they landed us on the beach for the purpose of cleansing the ship. But we are still ashore. They found it healthier for us.

I think I have mentioned to you before that we are laying here as the reserve. We expect to go aboard again. I can tell you we felt relieved when we got ashore once more. We were packed up in that ~~knxx~~ ship 7 days. We have plenty of fresh oysters here but we have to catch them ourselves. There are several large beds close by our camp. The weather has been rainy for the last few days. Fruit trees are in full bloom.

Before we were put ashore we were taken down to Fortress Monroe to be landed there, but General More (?) would not allow them to land us. I had a good view of the Monitor and also seen the smoke of the Merimack (Merrimac) laying beyond Swervel's Point. The fort is a grand old structure. I was sorry we could not get off the ship to see the inside of it.

There are 8 or 10 war vessels laying around. Also a French and an English men of war. We went back to our old anchorage the same evening. We do not know how long we lay here, but I am satisfied to lay here for a few weeks. It is pleasant.

I was glad to hear you had such a good job. I wish I could be with you to help to work, but I expect to be home ere long. The rebels are nearly played out and cannot hold out against George B. much longer. I should not be surprised if he would bag them at Yorktown. That would end the rebellion at the same place the Revolution was ended. With my love to you all I will close

Remaining Your Loving Son and Brother

E.W. Reed

P.S. Write soon. Direct as before.

P.S. My love to Sister Emma and William

Crab Point   May 2nd, 1862

Dear Parents, Brothers and Sisters:

            Being at leisure this evening I thought I would pen
a few lines to you, informing you that I am enjoying very good health and
it is my sincere wish and hope this will reach you all enjoying the same
great Blessing. We have had bully times since we are here. No drilling and
plenty to eat. Oysters and fish. We have fried oysters, soup stews, ~~xxxxxxxxxxx~~
in fact we use them all kinds of ways.

            News are scarce. We cannot rove about much. Our ships
are anchored in the creek or bay. I believe Cheseman's creek is the prin-
cipal one. I suppose you will know that New Orleans was taken by our forces
and is now occupied by Federal soldiers. Our prospects are brightening up
more every day. If McClellan takes Yorktown the war is ended, that is the
greater part of it. There may be a guerilla warfare carried on for a little
while. But that is soon squashed and they do not want all the soldiers to do
it. I must stop writing. The light is all (gone). My love to you all. Excuse the shortness of my letter. I merely wrote to let you know that I am
well. Write soon. I am anxious to hear from you.

                    Your Loving Son

                        E.W. Reed

P.S. This morning it is very pleasant. Myself, Dave Huber, Lent Huber, Joe
Morehiser, John Wetzel and a few more have got our quarters in a little old
log school house about 3/4 of a mile from camp.

May 13, 1862

Dear Parents, Brothers and Sisters:

   Being at leisure this morning I thought I would drop a few lines to you informing you that I am well as usual and I sincerely hope this will reach you all enjoying the same Great Blessing.

   Yesterday we again had a hard march of about 15 miles under a hot sun. We traveled faster than we have ever done and many of the men gave out under the pressure. I bet if our company should have marched into old Pine Grove yesterday afternoon, as we marched in a corn field to encamp, you would not have knowed the half of us. We were almost equal to the niggers, black and covered with dust from head to foot. But the river being near, we soon washed ourselves and felt considerably better.

   Nearly the whole army moved yesterday. The roads were all full. Our Regiment had the advance yesterday of our Brigade. McClellan has got the rebels right now. Yesterday I understand they sent in a flag of truce, asking for a cessation of hostilities for 15 days. But they see now that they are in a trap, and he will not give it to them. He will bag the whole of them and that settles the war.

   There is a report in camp that two Regiments of rebels were taken prisoners last evening about 3 miles from here. The niggers seem to enjoy it very much to see our coming down here. But I must bring my letter to a close. I have recieved no letter from you for two weeks now. I am anxious to hear from you at home. We do not get our mails regular now. We have recieved no mail for a week. Write soon and a good and long letter.

     Remaining Your Loving Son and Brother

       E.W. Reed

Direct as before

City Point, Va.

July 4, 1862

Dear Parents, Brothers and Sisters:

Having at last found leisure for a few moments I thought I would drop a few lines to you. I am still well and in good spirits and my only hope and desire is this will reach you all at home in the same good condition.

I have passed through many dangers .... James River. Some say it was a strategic movement. I do not know how it is, but this much I do know: That our army lost about 20,000 men and we are further from Richmond than we were. I ~~have~~ have no doubt the government will call for more troops, only do not let Andrew enlist. He would rue it. I have seen things that almost makes a man crazy to behold. Let no enthusiasm or nice promises lure him to do it. We were promised everything and have got nothing.

The regiment is ragged and worn out. Our First Lieutenant Elerich ~~was~~ was killed and several wounded. Uncle Israel got a slight wound. The bullet knocked off his cap and grazed his head. He did not leave the field but until evening it was a desperate battle. But the rebels had too many men for us, about 10 to 1 of us. The Pine Grove boys all escaped safe.

But I must close for this time. I hope you are all enjoying yourselves today. So with much love to you all I will stop. Write very soon. I am so anxious to hear from you.

Your Ever Loving Son

E.W. Reed

Direct as before.

July 6th, 1862

Turkey Creek(?)   B(ull) R(un), Va.

Dear Brother:

I write this letter two days later because I have more time now
than when I wrote the letter of the 4th. Thank God I am still well, and my only
wish and hope is this will reach you all at home the same.

I will endeavor to describe to you our whole march, and a detail
of things that happened after and the night before the battle of Mechanics-
ville. If you have read the account of the battle in the papers you will have
seen that the fight commenced Thursday at about 3 o'clock P.M., on the extreme
right.

That day we were in our camp near Fair Oaks. In the evening at
about 4 o'clock we got orders to get ready, light marching orders. But I think
                                           that
think I will have to explain what light orders mean nothing but haversack, and
canteen, accoutrements and gun. Well, at 6 o'clock we marched in front of the
picket lines, and there we were informed that we were to work. We worked all
night, digging a long entrenchment right under the very nose of the rebel pickets.

We had it finished until (by) morning and marched back to camp,
had hardly got our coffee when we were again ordered out. We marched to New
Bridge (?) and laid there about three hours, the fighting going on all the
time. Finally we got orders to march from there again and crossed the river.
Then we knew what was coming. We were almost dead until we got to the battle
field, you can think (imagine), not having not rested for 48 hours and eaten
very little. Everfirst

The first sight that drew our attention was the bringing of
                                  field,
so wounded out of the field, some shot in the head, others in the legs and
arms, and wounds of every description. But we did not stop and passed on
to the right. There were two men wounded passing around the field. We rested
behind a small hill for a few minutes. Our brigade being together, we cheered,
and then got orders to lay down. We had hardly done so when whizz came a can-

Camp Nougoant (?) August 8th, 1862

Dear Parents, Brothers and Sisters:

I will drop a few lines informing you that I am well, hoping these few lines may reach you all in the same good condition. There are no news here of any importance. The weather is very hot. We do not have to work quite so much any more. The redoubt is finished. The health of the troops was very bad for some time back. Many died. It is a little better again. When this month is around once, then we can look for better times. It is so hot just now that we have to have shades built over our tents, made of txigx leaves and twigs.

Yesterday was the first day we had bread since we left Alexandria. I hope we will get it for some time at least. Again I can tell you it tasted good. Dave Huber has just told me that the mail is about going off, so I will close, as I would like it, or the letter, to go off this evening. I have been looking for a letter xxx over eight days already, but none has come to hand. I am anxious to hear from you.

We got pay day this week. I concluded to keep their two months wages here this time. Write soon. You will please me by making use of the money I have at home. Give the little boys and girls a few cents now and then, and if Andrew wants to go out with the Band any place he can take some. Make the best use of it you can. There is no use having money laying still. I hope the war will not last long any more. My opinion is 6 or 8 months. Uncle Sam will pacify his children. Write long letters and often. It is the only consolation we chaps have.

I remain Your Loving Son and Brother

Erasmus W. Reed

Direct as usual

August 11th, 1862

Camp Near Harrison Landing

Dear Parents, Brothers and Sisters:

Your kind letter was recieved yesterday morning and gladly perused. I thought you had quite forgotten me. I had been looking for a letter for some time but I always like to have them better late than never. I am enhoying very good health. It is my sincere wish and hope this will reach you all in the same good condition.

There are not much news of any account going on here just now. We are under marching orders since yesterday. It is supposed that we will embark and go down the river. I hope we will not have to march on account of the hot weather. I suppose the whole army will be withdrawn from this position. At least we have every indications of such a move taking place. They have been shipping troops and artillery for some time already. It is my opinion that we will, that is if we embark, we will go back and ascend the Rapahanock and cooperate with Pope.

It is miserably hot here. We can hardly stand it any more. We are all glad if we can get a change. I wonder how the poor fellows are going to stand it, that just came or are coming out. We have not got quite so many deaths as we had a week ago. The men were dying whole sale for some time. I hope the new troops will be able to stand it.

The army is quite jolly to hear that enlisting progresses so finely. I heard this morning that the Old Keystone State had her quota in the field, I am glad to hear. I do not believe that there will be a man drafted for the six hundred thousand men. I am confident we will whip the rebels this fall yet. The boys are all glad to see that our government is waking up and taking the thing in earnest.

You will please not trouble yourselves if you do not recieve a letter from me for a week or two, because if we should happen to leave I may not have the chance to write until we are again settled at some place. I must close for this time. Write soon again. I send my love to you all.

E.W. Reed

P.S. Direct as before and give my respects to Uncles George, John, Jake and all the rest, and when you write again to Uncle Dave tell him to write to me. I would like to hear from him very much. Give him my directions. By Jingo, if we get up there I may have the chance to see the Old Boy.

Sharpsburg   September 20th, 1862

Dearest Parents, Brothers and Sisters:

Three cheers for the good news. The rebels are driven out of
Maryland into Virginia again, leaving many thousands of their dead and wounded ~~from~~ Also much of their artillery and baggage. Did I not tell you I
here.
would write you good news before long? We showed them what it was to come to
our States. Believe me you can hardly pass through a field or woods that
does not lay full of dead rebels still unburied, and I fear can never be
buried. The corpses are bloated and the smell is dreadful. The very air we
breathe around here is tinted with the dead smell.

I am still with the headquarters train and am well. My earnest
wishes are this will reach you all the same. Our army is still after the
rebs. There will be more fighting, but I believe the results will ~~terminate~~
be the
termination of the war. At least I believe it will be ended till winter. If
we get them on a good run, they will never reach Richmond with their army.
I know what retreating is. We had only 15 miles to retreat on the Chickahominy
and what an amount of men and property we lost. The rebs have over 1 hundred
miles to go. A few more weeks may bring about much. I hope through God's mercy
it will end the war. There had been fighting for over 8 days in Maryland.
Their army is much used up, while ours is filled more every day.

I must close. I must answer Emma and Bill's letter. Tell An-
he
drew ~~has~~ shall go soldiering as no other than State Militia. Then he does not
need to go out of the state. I think I have seen enough of the horrors of
war not to give unnecessary advice. I send my love to you all.

Your Loving Son

E.W. Reed

P.S. I have not recieved my shirt yet, but I suppose it will come in the next
mail. We only get a mail every three days. Write very soon. Isreal and John R
Reed are well. Give my regards to all the friends.

Dear Parents, Brothers and Sisters:

      Your letter dated the --- was recieved yesterday and gladly perused. I am still well and sincerely hope this will reach you all the same. There is still no change of affairs here except in weather. It commenced raining this morning and has been raining briskly ever since. I suppose we will have high water, as we used to say at home. I see in the papers you are having quite a time in Schuylkill County County caused by the draft. Well, it is no wonder that the County is getting stubborn. They have sent soldiers enough.

      I pity the poor fellows that were unlucky enough to be drafted in the Borough and Township of Pine Grove. The worst of the case is they must leave just about the time good living commences at home. They will find no fresh sausages, pudins and such with us fellows. Our hard bread is miserable that we got for the last 6 or 8 days. It is full of worms and weavels. I can tell you it goes pretty hard to grind such stuff in our stomachs, but we have none better so we must eat it. It strains pretty hard on a man's patriotism to be living as we do. I for one would see the country in a harder pinch than it ix now is before I would go soldiering again. Our pay master seems to have forgotten us. He has not been here yet. I recieved the three dollars you sent me. I mentioned it in my other letter which you had not recieved when you wrote your last.

      Yesterday our Division was reviewed. The troops looked well. General Brooks has superceded fix Slocum in command of the Division . I must close for this time. I only hope they will settle the war one way or the other this fall yet. Andrew may be glad that he took my advice in not enlisting. My love to you all. Write soon.

           Your Loving Son
              E.W. Reed

November 1st, 1862

In camp near Berlin, Maryland.

Dear Parents, Brothers and Sisters:

Your ~~kxkx~~ kind letter was recieved this evening. I was very glad to hear from you, e specially as it informed me of your good health. I am enjoying No. 1 good health and hope this may reach you all the same. We are on the move again and started from our camp near Bakersville yesterday morning at 5 o'clock and marched that day to the foot of South Mountain, and this morning we crossed the mountain at the same place where we had the battle about 1 month ago. The place is quiet now. There would hardly be any signs of a battle being fought there except the graves of the poor fellows who fell there and the cripples hopping about the village of Bergetsville. I do not know where we are going. Some think we will go to Washington and others that we again go to infernal Virginia. I would rather go to Washington. Of course we cannot expect to stay there. But any place rather than Virginia. I hate that place. I do not know what the reason is, but I suppose the hard times I had in that state makes it.

The weather is pleasant, neither too hot or too cold. Of course the nights are getting fresh. I believe we will get tough times this winter. The northern people had no rest until they had us on the move. I dread the consequence should we again have a reverse in Virginia. They do not seem to think or consider how heavy the task is they urge us to undertake. We all hope to be successful and even more so than the folks at home, because it is us that go through the hardships. Now the report is that the rebels have fallen back to Staunton about 1 hundred miles from here. For instance we should go there and be again beaten. Then for the hard times, with winter looking us in the face. But I hope such will not be the case. If they only let McClellan alone and not interfere in his plans, then all will be well. The expedition that go south may do good service. Our clothing is good, conesquently we must carry heavy knapsacks.

Some time ago there was an order issued that all men be-

ing absent in hospitals, from a certain date, they were to be stricken from
the rolls. Bill Snyder, Fred Syeese are among that number. I think Bill
will be home, if he is not already. They are discharged dishonorably, the
officers say. I must come to a close. I am in want of nothing just now. The
boots I do not want yet. I will send for them after while. I will perhaps
send for money in my next letter. We will not get paid until next month.
If we go to Washington I expect good times and it is my opinion the war will
be settled this winter. I send my love to you all. Write soon. Excuse bad
writing. I am tired from marching.

Your Loving Son and Brother

E.W. Reed

P.S. Direct as usual.

Andrew, I am glad you have got the band all right again. I have not got
time to write more to you or I would. I will write to that person as soon
as I get time. Write soon.

Your Brother

E.W. Reed

January 10th, 1863

In camp near White Oak Church, Va.

Dear Parents, Brothers and Sisters:

Your letter dated the 2nd came to hand yesterday. Its contents were perused with pleasure. I am glad to hear that you are all well and that you enjoyed yourselves over the Holidays. With us they were passed like any other day. With us the days are all alike, Sundays not excepted.

There is nothing new going on here. The weather has been extremely cold for several days, compeling us to sit around the fires all the time. The nights are passed rather uncomfortably. But the weather is better than I expected it to be. Until this time we have still done nothing in the way of building winter quarters. And I do not believe that the army will go into winter although we may lay at a place several weeks. The Western army is doing well. The papers, I see, are having a great time of it and already they announce that the end of the war is drawing near.

I differ a little with them on that subject. The war is not ended because our army has been sudcessful in the West, and I do not think it a very wise plan to inspire the nation with hopes which may be rocked (wrecked) by a simple reverse, and discourage them more then by simply taking the facts as they are. It is better to look the work before us in the face, because there is a large portion of it yet undone.

Let the government now do their duty. Let them arm the Nigers (Niggers as fast as they come into our lines, form them into regiments and make them fight for the freedom which our government has offered to them. At first our soldiers would not have liked the idea of having the Blacks help us to fight for the restoration of the Union. But now there is an addition made. The war is now for the Union and the freedom of the slaves. I for my part say, let the Nigers (Niggers) be put in the active field where they can be made useful, and not at landing stations. If they don't fight let them go back into slavery. What is the use of us risking our lives if they do not want to do something for themselves?

I must close for this time, hoping the dark clouds now hanging over us will soon disappear, and peace and prosperity once more xt reign supreme. Write soon. I send my love to you all and am

                    Your Affectionate Son

                         E.W. Reed

          Direct as usual

January 17th, 1863
Bell Plains, Va.

Dear Parents, Brothers and Sisters:

Your letter dated the 13th was recieved yesterday and perused with pleasure. I am well, and my sincere hope is this will reach you all the same at home. L noticed in your letter that my money arrived safe. There is nothing new going on here. The weather has been extremely cold for the last few days. We have been on duty here at this place for three days, building cord roy (corduroy) roads and a new landing.

You say in your letter that you had recieved no letter from me for 8 days. I cannot see what the matter is. But I think you will have recieved one of my letters that I wrote a few days ago. You also mentioned that Andrew was going to Reading to learn his trade. I wish in your next letter you would let me know what trade he is going to learn, and the conditions of his bargain. He must write to me every week at least. Also with whom he is going to learn/~~his~~ the trade.

Uncle Dave I have not seen for some time. Harrison Manwiller told me that Dave was cooking for the teamsters, so he is in no danger of getting into a fight. Isreal is well. If you need the money I have at home, use it. I must close for this time. Write soon again. I send my love to you all.

I am Your Affectionate Son

E.W. Reed

Direct as usual

On the road between Gettysburg and Chambersburg, Pa. .

Dear Parents, Brothers and Sisters:

I suppose you are anxious to know how I am getting along in these excitable times. I am well and all right. We have given the rebels the confoundedest thrashing at Gettysburg that they ever got They left fifteen thousand wounded in our hands. We captured a large number of prisoners and they are now retreating back as fast as they can, but we are close on their heels. We had a small skirmish with their rear guard last evening. Their loss is said to amount to thirty thousand and there is a good prospect of their losing as many more before they get back.

※※※※※※※

July 8th

In camp near Middletown, Md.

I will now endeavor to finish my letter which I commenced in Pennsylvania. We had one of the hardest marches that we ever made, having marched two whole nights and a day and a half steady. Last night we commenced crossing a mountain and it took us until nearly day light to get to the top. It was a very tedious march. What made it worse it commenced raining when we got to the foot of the mountain and rained steady until ten o'clock today. Maryland is almost as muddy as Virginia. I have not had a perfectly dry shirt on for ten days. It has rained more or less every day since we started from Fairfax Court House. But we do not mind it. The news are glorious all around.

I have heard that Brother Andrew is out with the militia. If you write to him tell him to write to me immediately. I can't write any more just now. I will give you all the news when we are a little more settled. I am enjoying very good health and trust this will find you all the same at home. I send my love to you all. Write soon.

I am your affectionate son

E. Reed

P.S. Did you get that money for Solly Moyer's wife and did you fix it all right? Address me 2nd Brigade Band, 1st Div. 6th Corps, % Capt. Stone, Wash-

(Part of an incomplete letter ◊

But I suppose it will take two or three days more fighting. I had almost forgot to mention that we took a quite smart lot of prisoners. Our Orderly Sergeant was wounded pretty bad and Charles Borger from ~~Fredrick~~ Friedensburg (?) slightly. That was the casualties we had in our company. Company R (?) lost 20 men. That was the most out of one company. We also took three pieces of artillery. Uncle Israel is well. John ReQd is sick. I must close for this time, hoping that I may be able to write you still better news in my next. I send my love to you all.

Your Loving Son

E.W. Reed

P.S. Direct as usual. I have still recieved no letter from you. It is now over two weeks. I am anxious to hear from you. We are about 7 miles from Harper's Ferry on top of the Blue Mountain. Give my respects to all friends. Write soon.

New Baltimore, Va.

August 6th, 1863

Dear Parents, Brothers and Sisters:

Your letter of the 4th came to hand a few minutes ago and found me enjoying good health. I trust this will reach you all in the same good condition at home. I was very much pleased to hear that you were getting along so fine, that you had everything so plenty and that Pap had a good job. When I hear such news from home I am always content.

I am also very glad to hear that Brother Andrew is or has returned home. I hope he will stop there. Of course in an emergency like the late one it is right for him to go. Now that he is home again he and Pap can lay in a good stock. Your account of the garden interested me very much. I wish I had a good mess of beans here. Now beans are scarce here. But the blackberries are plenty. I have had as much as I wanted to eat all along our route.

August 8th, 1963

I will now resume my letter and try to finish it this time. Yesterday we moved our camp a short distance after we had fixed up a nice place. But the General moved his head quarters to a house and the band of course had no alternative but to move also. In advantage of camp ground we did not lose much. There is a splendid shade tree here, which we appropriated to ourselves. The weather has been very hot some days. But still it is no comparison to what it was this time last year down on the Peninsula. Here in the mountains we have a cooling shower of rain almost every evening.

I see in your letter that Gus Snyder has been home and told you about a shirt I wanted. I had not intended that you should send it by mail. But I suppose he will be detained longer than we at first thought. Pap's likeness has not come to hand yet, but I may yet get it. The letter must be laying over some place. We expect to be paid before long. Hoping to hear from you soon I will close. My love to you all, I remain

Your Affectionate Son

E. Reed

August 29th, 1863 August 29th, 1863

New Baltimore, Va.

Dear Parents, Brothers and Sisters:

Your letter dated the 22nd came to hand. I had given up all hopes of getting a letter. It must be an awful trouble to write a few lines to let me know how you are getting along. Say for instance you write me a letter once a week, which will only take 15 minutes of your time, and I would always be informed how things go on at home. It is no pleasure to me to write three letters more or less until I recieve one. Of course I have more time to write than you have, I suppose. But still the few minutes it takes to write a letter you can spare. I would advise you to appoint a particular day in the week to write to me. Then I will get my letters regular. If Brother Andrew is too busy to write, then let one of the girls do it. It would give me more pleasure than anything else I can think of to recieve a letter from you once a week.

Our brigade is still occupying the same position as we did when I wrote my last letter. The weather is delightful during the day. The nights are beginning to get cool. We can buy plenty of vegetables from the farmers, so we make out to live pretty well. I see in your letter that our garden is yielding a good crop. I am glad to hear it. Perhaps I can be home this winter to help to eat some of them dried beans Mary was speaking of in her letter.

The band is getting along fine. We got three new members the other day from New York State. One plays a soprano, the other a tenor and the third bass. They are old musicians and make a great improvement in our squad. There is one more to come. He is to play solo alto. I think we will have a good band in a short time. They are all first rate fellows. But our leader is the best of all. I do not want to be under a better man than he is in all respects.

How is Doctor Dreher's family getting along? We used to be great friends and I would like to hear from them some times. To Uncle John I wrote long ago. But he was just kind enough not to answer my letter. I must close. But I had almost forgot to mention that I am enjoying very good health and hope this will reach you all the same. My love to you all at home. Write soon.

Your Affectionate Son

E.W. Reed

P.S. Send me some stamps and a thin sea weed fishing line. I want to use it for strings on the valves of my instrument. Let Andrew get them. He probably knows what I want.

August 29th, 1862

Fort Lyons (?), Alexandria, Va.

My Dear Parents, Brothers and Sisters:

I had nothing to do this evening so I thought I would drop a few lines to you informing you that I am very well and my earnest hope is this will reach you all in the same good condition. There have been considerable rumors afloat here for the last few days. One of the Brigade in our Division has gone up to Manassas and had a fight; I have not learned the particklars.

We have had a pretty good rest since we are here and I hope we will stop a few days longer. The weather is much more pleasant than on the Peninsula and we also have more to eat. We get bread since we are here. It tasted A No. 1. I can tell you being without bread so long, then getting it, it goes fine. Uncle Isreal is well, also John Reed. I must close for this time. It is time to go to sleep. I send my love to you all.

From Your Loving Son

E.W. Reed

Direct as usual. I will answer Sister Mary and Clementine's letter this week. Write soon. I am always anxious to hear from you.

September 3rd, 1862
Alexandria, Va.

Dear Parents, Brothers and Sisters:

I have just had a kind of a breakfast and will now drop a few lines to you, informing you that I am well, but completely wore out. We marched from Centreville to this place in 24 hours, and were in the meantime on picket a few hours at Fairfax. I am sorry to inform you that the battle was again lost. But our army withdrew in good order. I understand the papers blame our corps for the loss of the battle, but that is not so. We went out as quick and fast as we could. It was McDowell's corps that lost the Battle.

We reached the scene of the conflict a little after four o'clock when, just as we were going to pile in, McDowell's men gave way. They came out of the field helter skelter. Our Brigade formed across the road to keep the men that were not hurt back, but it was no go. So when they seen that they could not keep them back, we left them go. Hundreds of wounded passed us there. Nine out of ten were shot through the hands and arms. I seen only one with an arm entirely shot off. Our Brigade with two Batteries held the place until morning, when we were relieved by Reno's Division.

Our prospects look very poor just now. The rebs will try to get north, but they are not there yet. They are very jubilant just now. Let them be. We were so too, once. You will recollect that we were within four miles of Richmond at one time. Now we are at our own capital again. You may depend upon it that it will go the same way with them. They will never get north far. Every man in the army knows what the result would be. Our homes would be in danger. Some people think they can go right through now because they have been victorious for the last two (or) three months. But they do not understand it. The further they get from the base of their depot of supplies, the more troublesome they will find it.

I do not believe that this war will be settled by fighting. It will be a question of time. Our money will last longer than theirs. In a

great many places they are suffering from starvation. The letter dated the
29th and enclosed with this one I wrote before we left for Bull Run, but
did not get the chance to send it. I must close for this time, hoping this
will reach you all in the enjoyment of good health. Write soon. I send my
love to you all. My respects to all friends.

^{August}

        I Remain Your Loving Son and Brother

           E.W. Reed

Direct as usual

Sharpsburg, Md.

Sept. 20th, 1862

Dear Brother:

I recieved your letter three days ago but did not have the time
to answer it sooner. In the first place I must let you know the good news.
The rebels are whipped completely out of Maryland, after about 8 days fighting.
There are thousands of their dead still unburied, laying around the fields.
We took much of their artillery and baggage and any amount of prisoners. But
as to the exact amount of prisoners and artillery and other property, you will
know better than I do, because we have to look in the papers for that infor-
mation ourselves.

You may wonder how that is. Well I will tell you. Whore there
is an army of 150,000 to 180,000 men, one wing does not know what the other
is doing. All we know more than you is we are here when the battles take
place and can see the true effects of a battle. Yesterday I passed over
the battle field of the last day's fight on the right wing. I thought I
should have to throw the inside out of me. You ought to have seen the dead
rebels. In three large fields they were laying just as thick as they could.
They had been laying 24 hours already. The smell was horrible. I only seen
one or two that were white in the face. The faces of the others wore black
and bloated awfully. It was a terribly sad sight I can tell you. Where they
were trying to get over a fence, many of them were hanging half way across,
some laying on top of each other. I am getting more sick of it every time I
see it.

Take my <s>advice</s> and do not enlist under any considerations. Of
course in the state service, I can say nothing against. But do not go any
further than that. The state does not need her men. We are driving the rebs
home again faster than they came up. I must close for this time. Write soon x
and give my love to all at home. My respects to all the band.

I Remain Your Loving Brother

E.W. Reed

Wind Mill Point, Va.
February 28th, 1863

Dear Parents, Brothers and Sisters:

Being at leisure for a few moments I thought I
would xx drop a few lines to you, informing you that I am well. I trust this
may reach you all in the same good condition. I have no news to communicate
this time. We xxxx had a tremendous snow storm here a few days ago, but it
has since rained again and taken it all away, leaving us considerable mud.

We are still at work on different landings be-
tween Aquina Creek and Bell Plains. I like the place better every day. Our
quarters are comfortable and the rations good. We draw x ft bread four times
a week. The only thing I do not like very well is that we do not get our
mail regular. Yesterday we recieved the first mail in 10 days, and then
there was none in it for me from home. I recieved Billy and Georgy's letter
and (one) from Dave Huber and am much obliged fxx to them for it. Also the
valentine. I must close for this time. Write soon. Please tender my sincere
thanks to Uncles George and John for the tobacco they sent me. It just came
in the nick of time. I send my love to you all

And Remain Your Affectionate Son

E.W. Reed

Direct as usual

Mud Mill Point, Va.
February 16th, 1863

Dear Parents, Brothers and Sisters:

Your letter of the 7th came duly to hand. It's contents were perused with pleasure. The shirt you sent me also reached me and it fits me bully. In fact you could not have made it better if I had been at home. I did not know that the rates of postage were raised on such articles. Hereafter the Government will not make a fortune of me in that line. It is the soldiers they have to thank that they can collect such an ~~enormous~~ enormous sum in the Postage.

We are still doing duty here at this place. I have nothing new to communicate. It does not seem like being in the army here. It is very seldom that we hear drums, bugles, or even the discharge of a musket. It is my opinion that there will be a move made in the army ere long. I am satisfied. I would like to see Joe Hooker make his grand attempt, but I do not wish to be in the crowd.

We have fine times here. Of course we have to work every other day, but I do not mind that. I also understand we are to have soft bread as long as we are here, and we get an allowance of Grog every day. We also have more liberty. We can go where we please without a pass.

If you write to Sister Emma again tell them I would like to know why they do not answer my letter. I am enjoying very good health and trust this will reach you all the same at home. I must close. Write soon. Send me a few stamps.

I am Your Affectionate Son

E.W. Reed

Direct as usual

White Oak Church, Va.

April 3rd, 1863

Dear Parents, Brothers and Sisters:

Being at leisure this evening I thought I would drop a few lines to you. What is the reason you do not answer my letters? I am sure some of my letters must have reached you. We got a very poor mail just now. Today our Division was reviewed by Major General Hooker. The troops looked splendid, if anything better than last spring when we started out. They are all well clothed and well disciplined.

There has been a great change in the army since April. The army has again got the good old spirit and the enthusiasm of last spring is surely returning, and Hooker is getting to be a second McClellan. He has a fine army to back him. If it be God's will he must be successful.

Since Solly Moyer has again returned from home, I have been conversing with him, and in the course of our confab he told me that you had enquired how I was getting along, and that he told you that I had been sick last fall. So I thought it my duty to say a little on the subject. I had taken a pretty severe cold going through Maryland, but did not think it worth while to trouble you by writing it to you, as it was nothing serious. It is very natural to get a little cold now and then in the army, and especially through that campaign, because we did not use any tents and always slept in the fields. Therefore do not think that I will not let you know if I should be so unlucky as to get sick.

I am enjoying very good health and my earnest wish is this will reach you all in the same good condition. I send my love to you all. Write soon.

I Remain Your Dutiful and Affectionate Son

E.W. Reed

Direct Company B, 96th Regiment P.V.

2nd Brigade, Brooks Division, Washington, D.C.

White Oak Church, Va.
April 28th, 1863

Dear Parents, Brothers and Sisters:

Being at leisure for a few moments I concluded to drop a few lines to you, informing you that I am enjoying very good health, and my sincere hope is this will find you all in the same good condition. What is the reason you do not write? I have been looking for a letter for over a week now, but every mail I am disappointed. I cannot see what the matter is, whether the letters lay on the road or what it is. Anyhow I am anxious to hear from home.

I have nothing new to communicate. We expect to move soon. I suppose Andrew has told you that I am in the brigade band and am getting along first rate. The weather is splendid and the fruit trees are all in full blossom. It appears summer has fairly set in. Today we were paxmix payed off again for four months. I sent my money home with a Lieutenant of Company A. He lives in Pottsville and he will give the money to Captain Levi Huber. He will forward it to you. If you need money, use it.

I hope you will answer this letter soon. Let me know how the boys and girls are getting (along). Do not make your letters so short. Let me know all that is going on. John Eed and Isreal are both well and getting along fine. I will close by sending my love to you all. Remember me to all friends. Write soon.

I am Your Affectionate Son

E.W. Reed

Direct as usual. Let me know as soon as you get the money I sent.

May 17th, 1863

Camp near White Oak Church, Va.

Dear Parents, Brothers and Sisters:

I am at leisure, so thought I could do nothing better to pass away the time than by writing a few lines to you, and also because I have heard again that you made enquiries why I did not write. I wrote a letter to you a week ago which you will no doubt have recieved ere this.

It is Sunday today and it appears more so to me than it has since we left Camp Northumberland a year ago. We had very little benefit of the Sabbath through the past year, as we were most of the time either marching or working on that day. Divine service we have had none at all. Our chaplain left us long ago. Still I think we are just as well off as if he had been here.

We, the band, are camped alone in a beautiful pine woods several hundred yards from Head Quarters. I wish you could see us here. It is such a splendid little place. We are getting along fine and I think will make a
                                tuition
splendid band under the ~~direction~~ of Captain Stone. We are to be 24 men strong. I would not change my position for a 2nd Lieutenancy in a company. Here we are not ordered around by every and any body.

I have nothing new to communicate concerning the army. The men all seem to be in good spirits. Quite a number started for home, that is the two years troops. And (the)Pennsylvania Gallant nine months bounty men are also going home fast. I see that Charles Eck of our town is severely wounded. I am sorry for him and his family. Their time, that is the 129th Regiment, has nearly expired. I visited Eck several times since he is in the army. He seemed to lead a very pious life, which is a rare occurance in the army. I also visited Uncle Dave yesterday. He is getting along finely. This war has been the best thing in the world for him. The army is the place to make sober men. If Bill Snyder had stayed with the army I think it would have been better for him. I will close by sending you all my love. I am very well and hope you are all the (same). Write soon.

I am Your Affectionate Son

Andrew   May 22nd, 1863

Dear Brother:

Your letter and photograph came to hand last evening. I am sorry to hear by your letter that you are afflicted with a cow buncle (Carbuncle). I hope by the time this reaches you the cow buncle will have left you. I do not think it necessary for me to rehearse again what I have written to our parents as you can read the letter. I am glad to hear that the little (boys) are getting along well and fine. What are the girls doing? You never mention anything about them.

I showed your picture to the boys in the band and they complimented it very much, which I thankfully accepted. I think it is a very good picture of yourself. I do not remember right how you looked before I left, but think you have grown considerable in size and stoutness. I noticed your last letter was directed wrong again. I will give you a correct address now. Please copy it and keep it. Address me

                    2nd Brigade Band
                    1st Division 6th Corps
                    In care of Captain Stone
                    Washington, D.C.

Remember me to all my friends. My love to you and all in the family. Write soon.

                    Your Brother
                    E.W. Roed

P.S. Send me a few stamps.

May 22nd, 1863
In Camp near White Oak Church, Va.

Dear Parents, Brothers and Sisters:

I recieved a letter from you last evening dated the 17th and was glad to hear from you. This is now my fourth letter that I write inside of eight days. It appears by your letter that my first letter written immediately after the battle was either lost or has since come to hand. But be that as it will, I will again endeavor to relate to you where I was during the battle and what I was doing.

As soon as our corps commenced crossing the river, Brooks, the commander of our division, ordered the musicians to report to the division hospital for duty. In order to give you a correct idea what a division hospital is during a battle, I must explain. It is only a temporary affair, stationed in the rear of the corps, where the wounded get their first dressing. From there they are shipped off as fast as possible. The hospital moves as the army moves. If they advance the hospital advances, so in falling back it is the same.

Our duty was to put up the tents and take care of the wounded. We were not in much danger. A few shells came over our heads now and then, but that was nothing. It merely reminded us that there was a battle being fought. The doctors are nine of the pluckiest men and you see, we were under their command. Whenever a place would be pretty warm, they would move back and we would, of course, follow.

I had a splendid view of what was going on in front all the time. So now I suppose I have told you all that is necessary. You have no doubt read the accounts of the battle in the newspapers. I see in your letter that you again mention something about me being sick and not letting you know at times. I have written to you time and again that it was not so. You will sooner believe other persons than me. Of course I have felt indisposed at times, but thank God I have not been sick enough to trouble you by telling you. Another thing is, I am not childish enough to complain

or write home when I have only got a belly ache or a head ache. My picture
I had taken as soon as we came back from the march and on such occasions
we live rather poor. That was the reason it looked a little lean. I ought
to have waited until about this time. I think I would have made a better appearance.

The band is getting along finely. I have bully times. Yesterday A.M.
the aide de camp was here and took a list of our names to get us mustered out
of the regiments and mustered in as Brigade. We also made our first xxxxxxxx
serenade last evening at the General's quarters and were highly complimented
by him. I will close by saying that I am enjoying very good health and hope
this will reach you all the same. My love to you all. Write soon. I am

                    Your Affectionate Son
                        E.W. Reed

Fairfax Court House
June 19th, 1863

Dear Parents, Brothers and Sisters:

Your letter was recieved by me day before yesterday.
I did not have the opportunity to write sooner and now I have not got time
to write much. We are marching every day and have been for a week back, except today. You must not be surprised if you do not recieve a letter so soon
again, because I do not know when I will have the chance to write again my
until the rebels are driven back.

Enclosed you will find two dollars. You will please
put two dollars to it, which will make it four, and hand it to Solly Moyer's
wife at the earliest opportunity. I am enjoying very good health and I trust
this will find you all the same at home. Write soon. I send my love to you
all. Please do not neglect about that money. I am

Your Affectionate Son

E.W . Reed

The band is all right

September 19th, 1863

Culpeper Court House, Va.

Dear Parents, Brothers and Sisters:

        Your welcome letter dated the 7th reached me last evening. We left New Baltimore at 16th at 5 o'clock in the evening, and marched to Warrenton. From there we started and marched to this place the next day. It is a distance of some twenty odd miles. I was a pretty tough march. We forded two considerable streams of which I have not learned the names.

        I have no idea what the move will amount to. All I hope is that we will be successful. The weather is beginning to get cool, which will in some measure lighten the hardships of a vigorous campaign. By the tone of your letter it seems that there are some of my letters still on the road. A few days before we left New Baltimore I wrote a letter to Andrew and also one to you. I suppose, or at least hope, you will have recieved them by this time. I am sorry to hear that Sister Emma is sick. I hope her illness is not of a serious nature. I wonder why they don't write to me any more. I wrote them the last letter. But I will write to them again shortly. I have nothing more interesting to write so I will close. I am enjoying very good health and trust this will find you all the same at home. My love to you all and respects to friends. Write soon again.

        I am Your Affectionate Son

        E.W. Reed

Culpeper Court House, Va.
September 21st, 1863

Dear Brother:

In the other letter or last one you wrote you mentioned that you still had recieved no answer from me. I wrote one which I hope you will have recieved ere this. But at all events I concluded to write in case that should have been lost.

We are laying here at this place now for several days, for what purpose I do not know. All I know is that we made a very rapid march to get here. As far as I can learn there are two corps in this vicinity - ours and the 3rd, all laying along the Pike. The town of Culpeper is about two miles from here. Some of our boys have been down. They say it is a very nice little place.

The weather is cool, in fact the nights are almost too cool for comfort. The last two nights I slept very cold. But we must get used to it for this winter again. I only hope we can spend the winter a little further south than we did last winter. I should like it very much if our army could winter on the south side of the James River. Who knows? That may all come to xxxx pass yet.

The army as far as I can see is in fine spirits. Everybody seems willing to go through any hardships for the sake of winding up the war. The tide of battle has turned against the Rebels. It is with us to keep it in the ebb until the name of Rebellion is wiped out. Every body seems to have confidence in our Leader. General Meade has gained for himself a position in the confidence of the army of the xxxxxx Potomac second to none. May God grant it that he will always be successful.

Andrew, you at home have also a vigorous campaign in prospect. I mean the coming election. It is not necessary for me to advise you in regard to it, because without doubt you are on the right side, and that is for Curtai of course. If there are any of our connections who are not sure for Curtain, use your influence in converting them and get their xxxx votes polled in the

Loyal box. By all appearances, we in the army will not be allowed to vote. There is a certain Party in our state who seem to dread the results of a vote in the army, and well they may, if I am a judge of Tobacker. I must close for this time by stating that I am enjoying very good health and trust this will find all the same at home. Give my love to all in the family and write soon again.

                    I remain Your Affectionate Brother
                              E.W. Reed

        Address as usual

In Camp near Raccoon Ford, Rapidan River, Va.

October 7th, 1863

Dear Parents, Brothers and Sisters:

Your letter dated the second came to hand this evening and found me well. Our Corps left Culpeper Court House the day before yesterday, the fifth, to relieve the second Corps which had been here ever since our cavalry first advanced from Warrenton. The Rebels are on the other side of the river but fortifying themselves like fifty. Our pickets can see them plainly at work. Our camps are some ways back from the river. The pickets appear to be friendly, as there is not much firing between the two lines. I suppose the Rebels expect us to cross over and give them battle. But I am rather inclined to think they are digging for nothing, because I do not believe our army will attack them in such a strong position as the one they now occupy.

I see in your letter that you are expecting us home, and that rumor has even gone so far as to bring us to Harrisburg on the way to Pottsville. Well, that is good news enough. But we hardly believe it out here. But this much is true. The commander of the Regiment has been trying to get the Regiment ordered home to relieve a certain New Jersey Battalion and he may succeed yet. But there is nothing certain about it.

I suppose you have seen the order from the War Department concerning the reenlistment of Old Soldiers and paying them four hundred dollars. Well, they are at work here. I heard today that half of what is left of our Regiment has already reenlisted for the term of three more years. They can go to grass for all me. I will not reenlist if they offer ten times the bounty they now pay.

I am glad to see that you have got a new and good chob (job). Please let me know in your next what the work is. The weather is getting to be confounded cold nights. I suppose we will go into winter quarters before long. At least I hope they have not got the idea like last fall, that they can prosecute a winter campaign in Virginia. I think that has shown plain enough that it cannot be done. I must close for this time, hoping this will reach you all enjoying very good health. My love to all in the family. Write soon again.

I am Your Affectionate Son

E.W. Reed

P.S. In coming here we passed by the first Corps. Some of the boys in the company seen Harrison Manwiller and also enquired for Uncle Dave. He is all right. So are both John and Isreal.

Direct as Usual

December 21st, 1863

Camp Near Hazel River, Va.

Dear Parents, Brothers and Sisters:

Your letter of the 19th reached me this evening, having come through xxx in less than 48 hours. Through your letter I am informed that you sent off a box intended for me today. It may possibly reach me before Christmas, but I do not expect it until next week, so that I will at least have it for the New Year.

Gus Snyder got a box through in four days. Perhaps mine will come in that time, too. I have nothing new to communicate. Everybody is fixing up for a permanent stay this winter. The weather is changable - some days stormy and rain and other days clear and cold. Warm weather has played out, and I consider we are very lucky lucky in getting such good quarters. You need not be at all concerned about me in that respect.

They are granting furloughs through the army. I will try to come home on a visit this winter some time. Two men out of our band, one is off now, and also our leader. They will be back after Christmas. If I succeed in getting a furlough I mean to be home the latter part of February, but do not put too much reliance in it yet, because I do not want to disappoint you. I will try my best to come. Love and write soon.

Your Affectionate Son

E.W. Reed

Hazel River, Va.
December 24th, 1863

Dear Parents, Brothers and Sisters:

This letter is to inform you that the box you sent me came to hand this evening, which you will observe by the date of my letter it is Christmas Eve. I am very much obliged for the present and very well pleased with it. I am sorry to inform you that one of the bottles of wine had bursted. The other two were safe and also all the other things.

Yesterday we had a big time. General Bartlett was presented with a gird (?)* watch and apauletts (epaulets) by the officers of the Brigade. The whole crowd was drunk. We expect General Bartlett back in our Brigade again He was up in the Regiment and spoke to each company separately, that is he made a speech to them.

The weather has been exceedingly cold for the past few days. But this far we have had but very little snows. There is nothing new going on here. The granting of furloughs has been stopped for a short time, I suppose on account of the reenlistment of Veterans. If 2/3 of an old Regiment reenlists they will be sent North to be recruited up to the required number. It appears that such Regiments take up all the spare transportation. So as soon as they are all shipped off, I think they will again grant furloughs.

I am well and hope this will find you all in the same good condition. I will close by sending you all my love and wishing you a very happy Christmas. Write soon.

I Remain Your Affectionate Son

E.W. Reed

* Webster's International Dictionary gives as a synonym for the word Gird, "Enclosed." That is the closest definition I could find that would be applicable as an adjective describing a type of watch. *A later clerk a watch maker who said it was a watch whose lid flew open when one pressed on the winder of the watch.*

                                     Hazel River Va.

                                     Dec. 31st, 1863

Beloved Parents:

          Yours of the 29th came to hand this evening and found me
enjoying very good health. I trust this may find you all in the same good
condition. I was happy to hear that you spent a happy Christmas. It is almost
12 o'clock so I may as well wish you all a happy New Year.

                                     Jan. 1st, 1864

          I was interrupted last year in writing this letter, so I
will finish in the New Year. The Holidays are about over and I have enjoyed
them as well as can be expected in the army. I have had good health and that
is all a soldier need ask for.

          My box you sent me came in good season and I enjoyed the
contents hugely. This morning we had orders to move at a moment's notice, by
rail to Washington and from there to Harper's Ferry. But I suppose things
turned out favorably there, as we need not go, and you may well think that
I am glad. I do not want to leave my present quarters in a hurry.

          Yesterday it was raining all day, and today it was bitter
cold. I suppose you have snow at home and probably Maj. Benawitz has left
the gate standing open in North Pine Grove, which is the cause of it being
so cold here. I will close by sending my love to you, and once more wishing
you all a Happy New Year. Write soon. I am

                    Your Affectionate Son

                         E.W. Reed .

Dear Parents, Brothers and Sisters:

Your very kind letter reached me this evening and was perused
with pleasure and satisfaction. Indeed I must give you the compliment of
saying that you can excel Brother Andrew in writing a letter. Only I find
a few words incorrectly spelled, but they are few. I merely notice this in
my letter, merely for your improvement. One of your letters has more news
than four of Andrew's. I am glad to hear of the termination of Sister Clementine's affair with that fellow. I am very happy to hear that wages are so
good for mechanics. Indeed I fairly ache to be at home and help Father and
Andrew. I hope wages will continue so until I come home.

There is nothing new going on here. We had a very heavy snow
storm the day before yesterday. The snow lay about six inches deep in a
level. That is the deepest we have had this winter. Today it has been quite
pleasant and the snow has almost disappeared. Snow never lays so long here
as it does at home. One sunny day will melt the deepest snow and in the
place where you have good sleighing we have mud. But thanks to Colonel Up-
ton for choosing us such a good camping place, where we experience very little
inconvenience from any and all kind of weathers. Few troops in the Army of the
Potomac can boast of such a camping place as we have got and especially some
of the new troops who came out last fall. I have observed in some of their
camps that they must fare rather hard. After they are out a year longer they
will learn to make themselves more comfortable.

Our Regiment this evening recieved 37 recruits. I was up when
they came, but did not see one face that I recognized. It was fun to see the
Regiment, that is the old boys, crowd around them and hold an inspection
over them. What I seen of them they seem to be a pretty good crowd of men.

I am glad to hear that the well turns out to be so good, and
especially the water. There is nothing better than to have a well of good

water. We were payed off today. I will send some money home in a few days.
I do not like to trust it in the mail immediately after pay day. I am enjoying very good health and trust this will find you all the same at home. I was
surprised to hear that Uncle Jake had enlisted. Please give my respects to
Dr. Dreher and all other acquaintances. My love to all in the family. Write
soon again.

                    Your Affectionate Brother

                           E. Reed

P.S. To Sister Mary: Please let me know what part of the house you intend to
rent away.

Dear Parents, Brothers and Sisters:

Your very welcome letter came to hand last evening and was perused with pleasure, only I was sorry to hear that Father was unwell. I hope by the time this reaches you he will be fully recovered. I am enjoying very good health and trust this will find you all the same.

There is nothing new going on here. The weather is very unpleasant, continually raining or snowing. The river has raised very much and the bridge that our fatigue squads and Pioneers had built was swept away. The pontoon bridge was saved through the exertions of the Engineer Corps or we would have been entirely cut off from the rest of the Army. We had been under the impression that the Army would move this month. But I think it hardly probable now. The indications are that this bad weather we are now having will last through this entire month. I am very well satisfied to stop here, as long as the weather is so unsettled.

We have not much to do now. Our only duty is to practice in the band room and occasionally at Head Quarters if the weather permits. I am happy to hear that Uncle Harry has bought a house. And bully for the little boys and their lime kiln. Please let me know in your next whether you recieved some money that I sent home. I will close for this time, once more hoping this will find you all well. I send my love to you all and respects to friends. Write soon again.

I am Your Affectionate Son

E.W. Reed

Near Spottsylvania Court House
May 11th, 1864

Dear Parents, Brothers and Sisters:

This letter I may possibly get through with one of the wounded going to Washington. This is the 7th day that our army has been fighting and this far it has been the severest battle of the war. Company B has been very unlucky. I will give you the list as far as I know. Solomon Moyer, Gust Snyder, Paul Parr, John Harvey, Vick Dubbs, Bill Leffler, Bill Rinewohl, Dan Benawitz are missing. They do not know what became of them. John Reed they think is dead. I cannot inform you for certain. The company lost 17 in all. The rest that I have not mentioned are from other places.

I am well. The only time that we, the band, were under fire was the first day. The battle commenced at Mine Run (?) and has finally got down to this place. I have seen a great many prisoners come in. Our loss in killed and wounded is heavy. The battle is still undecided. The general (word) is that we will clean them out. Hoping this will reach/and find you all well, I will close. My love to you all.

Your Affectionate Son

XXXXXXXXXX E. Reed

Head Quarters 2nd Brigade
Tuesday Evening, May 2nd, 1864

Dear Parents, Brothers and Sisters:

We are going to march tomorrow morning so I thought I would drop a few lines to you. Our communications may be stopped so you will know what the matter is if I do not write.

If we get the rebel army started I will have very little time to write. I am enjoying excellent health, and trust this will reach you all the same. The weather is pretty cold. But we feel it more because we lived in such good houses this winter. My love to you all. Hoping to hear from you soon I am

Your Affectionate Son

E. Reed

May 21st, 1864

Seven miles from Mechanicsville on the Peninsula

I have just learned that there is a mail going out, so I will drop a few lines to you. We recieved a mail last night, but I was very much disappointed indeed when I opened my letters and found there was none from home. Why don't you write? We get the mail at every chance they have to send it to us. I have only a few minutes time to write, therefore cannot give you all the particulars that happened since I last wrote to you.

Bill Rinewohl is dead. The boys in the Company buried him. He was still laying at the rifle pit that they had charged. He was shot through the head. John Reed and Dan Ronawitz were supposed to be dead, too, but they could not find their bodies, so in all probability they are taken prisoners. Also Frank Umbenhower. Our line of battle now is near and around Mechanics-ville, and there is considerable fighting all along the lines. I expect we will siege Richmond again shortly.

I talked with some of our cavalry that had been near Richmond and got some of their papers. One of them told me that he seen an article in which they stated that Grant was falling back all the time and that our loss was seventy thousand. But the folks around here cannot imagine what Grant is falling back toward Richmond for, with only 30,000. I presume they are begin-ning to smell a rat. Our Army is today as strong or stronger than it was when we started from winter quarters. Our Brigade has got a Regiment of heavy artil-lery numbering eighteen hundred.

I am enjoying very good health and trust this will find you all the same. When you write give me all the news. Whenever I get the chance I will write you all that happened this month, that is, as far as I know. There has been fighting more or less every single day this month. My love to all at home.

I am Your Affectionate Son

. E.W. Reed

Boliver Heights, Va.
July 30th, 1864

My Dear Parents:

Dick Soebell recieved a letter from home this morning from which I learn that it is reported around there that I am sick, in fact verry low.

I am happy to inform you that I am enjoying excelleht health. I had been verry unhealthy while we were down at Petersburg. But since we came to Maryland and the upper Potomac I am all right again. I hope Father has not started on such a wild goose chase as to find the 6th corps, which is every where and no where.At the present moment we are laying still. Fifteen minutes from now we may be on the march, and this evening, with good luck, you might find us 15 or 20 miles from here. That is our style of living now a days.

I presume you have heard that John Reed is alive, but a prisoner in Richmond. He had been wounded and is still in the hospital. Our corps was laying around Washington a few days, and while there was payed off. I was rather unlucky. I got no pay. I heard that Hen Heinz and Bill More were in Washington, so I and Dick started off in the morning to visit them and while we were gone our Regiment was payed off and we did not get any money. Well I do not care. I would just as leave wait a few weeks and get my whole pile together.

The postman is coming around so I must ~~bring~~ hurry and close. I hope this will find you all as well as it leaves me. Write soon.

Your Affectionate Son

E, W. Reed

Camp Franklin

Dear Sister Mary:

Your letter was recieved (with) great pleasure. I was glad to hear that you were well and going to school. That is the best thing you can do. Get all the knowledge you can because you will never rue it.

I suppose you have got fine times in school playing. But don't play too much and you will learn so much the more. I have not much to write because I have written everything in in Father and Mother's letter. So I will close remaining

Your Brother

E.W. Reed

~~XXHXWTAXBAXEFEAXSXHAXHIXMTXXGAWAXHXTIXHXI~~

P.S. I expect Andrew to be a pretty good musician till I come home.

(The following letter is on the reverse side of the stationary.)

Camp Franklin

Dear Sister Clementine:

Your letter was also gladly recieved. That to hear that you were well, it always makes me ~~fxk~~ feel good to hear that you are all well at home. Be a good girl and improve all your spare time you have in studying, because you will need it, especially writing, spelling and grammar. But also mind your work, so that your employers are satisfied with you. But I must close I will have to write two or three letters more. Give my love to Eliza and the boys, Black ----, Michael and George and little Ellie. Sister Emma, if God spares my life I will visit you when I come home. Then look out for longer. My respects to your husband.

E.W. Reed

Part of an incomplete letter

in the band. I will also let you know that I resigned my post as corporal, because they pay only 13 dollars a month. Therefore I would sooner be a private than corporal. We have recieved no pay yet, but we expect our money daily.

If we get it before this month is out, we will only get two month's pay, and then again the 5th of next month we will get the other two months. And if we don't get paid till the fifth of month we will get 4 months pay. Then I can send you 40 dollars or more. Therefore you can look for money soon. But I must come to a close. I send you all my love at home. One thing sure, the general opinion around here and Washington is that the war won't last long any more. Answer soon, and let me know all the news. My respects to my friends.

From Your Affectionate Son and Brother

Erasmus W. Reed

Write soon. Direct to me Co. B, 96th Regiment, P.V. in care of Captain P. S(?) Filbert, Alexandria, Fairfax County, Va.

P.S. Only don't believe the Eckles affair.

We had sour craut (sauer kraut) for dinner the other day, which was sent from Schuylkill County. And about coming home. That is impossible till Christmas, because there won't be no furloughs issued will March. Then I guess the war will be over. That is the general belief around here. Our naval expeditions are troubling them (the rebels) rather much. The war has caused much destruction in Virginia already. All around where we are the houses are vacated, and some splendid houses too, I can tell you. The woods are all cut down. There are two or three fort's near to us. Our beds are as comfortable as can be expected under the circumstances, But no more for this time.

Direct your letter to Washington, D.C., Camp Kendale Green, in care
of Captain Filbert, Company B, 96th Regiment.

                                        Camp Kendale

                                        Mr. John Rehrer

Dear Uncle:

         I will pen you this short note to let you know that I am well
and I hope you are all the same at home. You can't expect a big letter from
me this time, because I have got no paper nor means to send letters.

         You told me to write if I wanted some of the above named arti-
cles I should write to you. Therefore you will please send me the writing
materials. Tell my parents that I am well and like it first rate yet. I
will write to them before long. As soon as you will send me the papers I will
let you all know how we are getting along. We did not get any money yet. So
no more this time. Give my love to my folks at home, also Aunt Marry.

                          From Your Affectionate Nephew

                          Erasmus W. Reed.